WILMSLOW

THROUGH TIME

Vanessa Greatorex

AMBERLEY PUBLISHING

Quiz Time

Cheshire is famous for its black-and-white houses. Award yourself a gold star if you can identify this one. Flummoxed? Keep your eyes open when you're out and about in the Wilmslow area, and you might just spot it. Have fun!

First published 2013

Amberley Publishing
The Hill, Stroud
Gloucestershire, GL5 4EP

www.amberley-books.com

Copyright © Vanessa Greatorex, 2013

The right of Vanessa Greatorex to be identified as the Author of this work has been asserted in accordance with the Copyrights, Designs and Patents Act 1988.

ISBN 978 1 4456 0868 6

British Library Cataloguing in Publication Data.
A catalogue record for this book is available from the British Library.

Typeset in 9.5pt on 12pt Celeste.
Typesetting by Amberley Publishing.
Printed in the UK.

Introduction

Wilmslow's location has been the key to its development; on the Cheshire plain (handy for raising livestock), between two rivers – the fast-flowing Bollin and the Dean (easy access to water) – and cheek-by-jowl with the peat bogs of Lindow Moss.

These bogs famously precipitated the best-known instance of prehistoric human activity in the area – a macabre case of violent death which is usually interpreted as ritual sacrifice (for more of the gory details, turn to p. 96). Radiocarbon dating confirms that the victim was a well-groomed Iron Age man, who met his end roughly around 1 BC. What is less well-known is that people were living nearby a good deal earlier. Two Bronze Age urns containing cremated bones were found by railway workers when the viaduct over the Bollin was constructed in the 1840s, and a Bronze Age settlement was excavated when the second runway was built at Manchester Airport.

In fact, even Wilmslow's name may contain evidence of its Bronze Age beginnings. According to linguistic experts, it's is a corruption of the Anglo-Saxon phrase *Wighelm's hlaw*. The identity of Wighelm is a complete mystery. He could have been an Anglo-Saxon settler or a legendary figure of local importance. His *hlaw* (meaning 'mound') may have been a Bronze Age tumulus (though archaeological evidence for such a feature has yet to be found), or simply a hill. In truth, the latter is more likely – most '-low' names in Cheshire are associated with high ground rather than burial mounds.

The fact that the place-name elements are Anglo-Saxon suggests that a permanent community was based at Wilmslow before the Norman Conquest, even though it wasn't mentioned in the Domesday Book (many historians believe this omission occurred because Wilmslow was amalgamated with other lands held by the Earl of Chester when the survey was undertaken in 1086).

Documentary evidence of 'Wylmeslowe' dates from the late thirteenth century, when the locally influential Fitton family financed the construction of the church. To begin with, Wilmslow just denoted the land around the church and churchyard, and the ancient parish served by them. This originally consisted of four sprawling townships – Bollin Fee, Pownall Fee, Fulshaw and Chorley – which incorporated various hamlets at places like Dean Row. Boundary changes subsequently occurred, and the name Wilmslow was applied to both the evolving town and adjacent areas.

The parish's inhabitants were mostly engaged in farming until the eighteenth century, when the textile industry took off in Cheshire. Stretches of the River Bollin were ideal for powering mills, a factor exploited at nearby Styal, Bollington, Macclesfield, and in Wilmslow itself. Cotton and silk were produced at Carrs Mill, velvet was made in cutting workshops, and there was a demand for home-based handloom weavers and button-makers. This brought newcomers to the area, but many people remained closer to poverty than affluence until the coming of the railway.

Just 11 miles south of Manchester, Wilmslow's rural vistas attracted wealthy nineteenth-century industrialists who wanted to combine gracious living with easy access to their workplaces. This led to the creation of an infrastructure that allowed the town's location to be exploited to the full. Pick the right train, and you can be at Manchester in twenty-two minutes, Crewe in sixteen, or London in under two hours. The centre of Wilmslow is only 3 miles from the M56, and 5 miles from Manchester Airport, giving the town better access to international destinations than Manchester itself enjoys. Entrepreneurs, actors, footballers and legions of commuters have all succumbed to the lure of such convenience. From a rural backwater with scary prehistoric rituals, Wilmslow has become a best-of-both-worlds sweet spot, close to the countryside, big enough to offer a good range of facilities, yet firmly connected to the rest of Britain and beyond.

Acknowledgements

Many people, known and unknown, alive and long dead, have assisted in the compilation of this book. Thanks are especially due to: Joe Pettican for commissioning it and answering a multitude of questions with patience, promptitude and courtesy; all the photographers of the vintage pictures; Rosanna Roskilly for assistance on photography shoots; Linda Clarke and her colleagues at Cheshire Archives and Local Studies for access to Cheshire's collection of vintage photographs and permission to reproduce them; Stephen Roskilly for helpful observations on the pre-publication draft; Chris Sutherns of the British Museum for ultra efficiency; Denise Soussi, Charlie Cook, Ronnie Dykstra and Denovan Nowell of Wilmslow Green Room Society; Kristina Heath and Denis Hogan of Hyde's Brewery; Georgina Robinson and her sister Val; Paul Ackerley; Shaun Green; Alastair and Christine King; June Kirwin; the staff of Wilmslow Library; and anyone who knowingly or otherwise appeared in one of the photographs. Image of Lindow Man: © The Trustees of the British Museum. All rights reserved.

About the Author

Vanessa Greatorex is a freelance writer, editor and local historian who has lived in Cheshire for over thirty years and grew up in the vicinity of Wilmslow. Her back list includes *Robin Hood: Birth of a Legend*, a long-running series on place-names in *Cheshire Life*, and a couple of historical short stories. A member of the Chester Society for Landscape History, the English Place-Name Society and the Council for British Archaeology North West, she has three degrees – in English, Medieval Studies, and Landscape, Heritage & Society – and is currently conducting doctoral research into crime and disorder in medieval Chester. *Wilmslow Through Time* is her first book.

Transport, 1920s and 2012

In the 1920s, it was the prospect of an outing in Syd Jackson's charabanc that filled local residents with excited anticipation. Nowadays luxury super cars at the Wilmslow Motor Show appear to have a magnetic effect on men and boys, but alloy wheels and shiny red paint hold scant allure for the women and girl on the left.

Alderley Road/Water Lane, 1950s and 2012

After isolated trials, zebra crossings were rolled out at a thousand locations in England in 1949. Never a stranger to innovation, Wilmslow was at the forefront of improving safety, with its pedestrians able to benefit from a zebra crossing at the Alderley Road/Water Lane junction by the 1950s. It has now been superseded by a pelican crossing – but note how little the appearance of the shops on the right has changed over time.

Water Lane, 1978 and 2012

A bread strike caused queues to form in Water Lane when the winds of discontent blew in the 1970s. Now the pavements are occupied by Continental-style cafés, and the queues are more likely to be of traffic than frustrated shoppers in search of the staff of life.

Water Lane, 1977 and 2012
The Army Cadet Band was a stirring sight at the top of Water Lane in 1977. At the same spot thirty-five years later, race marshals take a breather between directing cyclists, while the erstwhile corset salon now sells upmarket shoes and designer handbags.

Water Lane, 1978 and 2012

Health and safety officials would doubtless be aghast today, but in the 1970s the impressive balancing skills of these daredevil workmen provided an an equally impressive bird's eye view of Water Lane (sporadically known as Little Venice because of its former propensity to flood). Life on the ground forty years on just doesn't have the same heart-stopping impact, no matter where you stand...

Methodist Chapel, Water Lane, 2012 and 1960s
Methodists have been worshipping in Water Lane for over 200 years, though not always on the same site. The Wesleyan chapel (*below*) was built in the 1880s to replace the 1798 chapel and Sunday school located further down the street, and could accommodate a congregation of 500. Demolition followed before it could celebrate its centenary. The new Methodist church opened in 1986.

Society of Friends Meeting House, Water Lane, *c.* 1950s and 2012

The Religious Society of Friends (also known as Quakers) was founded in 1652 by weaver's son George Fox, who preached that everyone could communicate directly with God without the need for priests. Registers of Wilmslow's Quakers date back to 1654, but the current meeting house on Water Lane was not built until 1830. Apart from a fresh lick of paint on the door, its façade has changed little over the decades – a striking contrast to the fortunes of the Methodist chapels.

Grove Avenue, 1920s and 2012

Wilmslow Preparatory School for Girls was founded in Grove Avenue in 1909, and still occupies the same site. In the 1920s the Conservative Club was on the corner with Grove Street, but is now further down the avenue. While many of the premises have changed over the decades, trees and dog-walkers would appear to be a permanent fixture.

Grove Street Jaw-Droppers, 1970s and 2012

A camel in Wilmslow? This photograph from the 1970s is impossible to replicate, but far too fascinating to omit. Note the lady on the pavement, whose incredulity at seeing exotic livestock in Grove Street must have been mirrored on many faces that day. In more recent times, longevity has doubtless dulled the impact of the iconic building on the corner but, more reminiscent of a seaside pavilion than a bank, in its own way it's just as much of an out-of-place curiosity as the camel.

Grove Street, *c.* 1900 and 2012
Its only shop a grocery on the corner, Grove Street was once part of the turnpike road to Manchester. Great was the glee when the toll bar at its entrance was removed in 1877, liberating locals from the necessity of paying three pence per wheel to go from one side of town to the other. The number of shops burgeoned, necessitating waiting restrictions in the 1950s and pedestrianisation a few decades later.

Grove Street, 1920s, 1970s and 2012

This is the view from the other end of Grove Street. Thanks to the pedestrianisation, the character of the street today seems more akin to that of the 1920s than of the 1970s (*inset*), when there was a constant flow of cars.

Bank Square, 2012 and *c.* 1900

Choose the right moment and Bank Square is as free from bustle today as it was in 1900. Now a bar, the attention-grabbing building with the clock and the cupola was originally the Union Bank of Manchester. However, the square's name is not derived from the financial establishment, but originates from its position on a slope, or bank, leading down to the church and up to the station.

Bank Square, *c.* 1900 and 2012

For 120 years (1856–1976) the curved lines of Walter Shields Clegg's drapery graced the corner of Bank Square. In the nineteenth century its own seamstresses and tailors made ladies' and children's clothes to order on the three-storey premises. The angularity of the current frontage is arguably less pleasing to the eye, but possesses an aggressive modernity which is perhaps more in keeping with the cutting-edge audio-visual merchandise sold there now.

Bank Square, 1911 and 2012
To celebrate the Coronation of George V in 1911, bunting decked the whole of Bank Square and a fountain graced the centre. During Queen Elizabeth II's Diamond Jubilee 101 years later, individual businesses took the lead in flying the flag and nothing was permitted to hinder the free flow of traffic.

Royal Celebrations, 2012 and 1902

The Coronation of Edward I was celebrated in full patriotic style in 1902, with flags and bunting festooned across Grove Street. Eye-catching red, white-and-blue displays – like Daniel Footwear's in Alderley Road – similarly dominated shop windows during Elizabeth II's Diamond Jubilee celebrations in June 2012.

Royal celebrations, c. 1911 and 1977

Flags were out again in Grove Street for George V's Coronation in 1911. Note the extraordinary number of bicycles, perhaps belonging to local members of the Clarion Cycling Club, formed nationally in 1895 and still going strong today. Six decades after the Georgian celebrations, it was a magnificently crafted barge which won the float competition at Elizabeth II's Silver Jubilee parade.

Jubilee Celebrations, Carrs Park, 1977 and 2012

Carrs Park was a focal point for both the Silver and the Diamond Jubilee celebrations of Elizabeth II's reign. On both occasions an elevated viewpoint was on offer – but the vibrant elasticity of the twenty-first-century bouncy castle seems positively tame compared with the vertiginous climbing frame of the 1970s.

Church Street, 1890s and 2012

Despite its fine church, Wilmslow's main street was not a prosperous location in the nineteenth century. Water was obtained from the pump on the right and, until 1860, an entry near the thatched cottages on the left led to Dungeon Walk, location of the town's two-cell lock-up. The Victorian writer Andrew Pearson described it as dismal, damp and loathsome, 'only fit for newts, toads and other vermin'.

George & Dragon, Church Street, 1979 and 2012

The George & Dragon was built in the early 1800s on the site of the Old George, an eighteenth-century alehouse. A butcher travelled over from Derbyshire once a week to sell mutton outside the pub at four pence a pound; whether the landlord got a discount is not recorded. The pub's twentieth-century car park was on the site of the thatched cottages shown on the facing page. Disused and in a poor state of repair in the early twenty-first century, the building now enjoys a new lease of life as offices.

Shopping in Church Street, 1965 and 2012

Church Street was Wilmslow's main shopping area in the nineteenth century. Its outdoor market was still going strong in the 1960s, when respectable housewives wore knee-length skirts and favoured sensible short hair-dos. Today's supermarket is partly located on the site of the Drill Hall, opened in 1877 as a training venue for local military volunteers. By the start of the First World War it had become the headquarters of the 7th Battalion Cheshire Regiment and was also used for dances.

Remembrance Sunday, 1979 and 2012

Men of Wilmslow died in action during both World Wars, and the town has not forgotten their sacrifice. Military bands, Army and Air Force cadets, policemen, members of the Royal British Legion, Scouts, Guides and citizens of all ages take pride in honouring the fallen every November with parades to and from the church and the war memorial.

War Memorial, Opening Ceremony 1969 and Remembrance Sunday 2012
The Memorial Gardens were opened in 1950 to commemorate the servicemen killed in the two World Wars. The cenotaph – originally located in Little Lindow and listing the 177 men of Wilmslow who died in the First World War – did not arrive for another nineteen years. A separate stone memorial commemorates the forty-eight men who fell in the Second World War.

St Bartholomew's Church, *c.* 1895 and 2012

Wilmslow's oldest building is the parish church, dedicated to St Bartholomew and first documented in 1246. Its crypt dates from around 1300, but much of the current building is sixteenth century, and there have been various alterations since then. The above picture was taken shortly before the top of the tower was redesigned in 1898. Note the majestic gateposts and the sweep of cobbles in front, where markets were held after the Second World War.

Lych-gate,
c. 1905 and 2012
The gateposts (shown on the previous page) were replaced in 1904 by a lych-gate. Traditionally the seat-level stone shelves either side were designed to accommodate a bier, giving coffin-bearers a respite while mourners assembled for the funeral service. The church itself was built by thirteenth-century scions of the Fitton family of Bollin, one of whom – Roger Phytun – served as priest. Nowadays dedicated volunteers spend several hours a week keeping the church spick and span.

St Bartholomew's Church, *c.* 1910 and 2012
Today trees make it impossible to take pictures from the angle chosen by the Edwardian photographer, so below is the nearest equivalent. Note that the houses – many of them inhabited by handloom weavers in Victorian times – have been demolished and replaced with the Memorial Gardens.

Churchyard, Twentieth Century and 2012

Although the churchyard boasts some of Cheshire's earliest gravestones, dating back to 1596, this did not inhibit the twentieth-century workmen instructed to lay a new path between the lych-gate and the south porch. Inside the church, on the chancel floor, lies another ancient memorial – the county's oldest brass, dating from 1460 and depicting Sir Robert del Booth and his wife, Douce.

Chancel Lane, 2012 and *c.* 1900

In 1900 some of the Chancel Lane dwellings opposite the church were looking decidedly the worse for wear. The large house at the front, signposted in the photograph as the premises of a boot and shoemaker, is billed as the Old Rectory in some sources, though it is hard to find original documentation to prove this. Beyond the Memorial Gardens today a delightful green oasis of grass and trees faces the church.

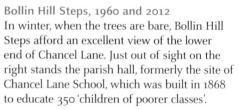

Bollin Hill Steps, 1960 and 2012
In winter, when the trees are bare, Bollin Hill Steps afford an excellent view of the lower end of Chancel Lane. Just out of sight on the right stands the parish hall, formerly the site of Chancel Lane School, which was built in 1868 to educate 350 'children of poorer classes'.

Bollin Hill Steps, 1960 and 2012

It's good to know that half a century doesn't always make much difference. Time of year aside, Bollin Hill Steps look almost the same in 2012 as they did in 1960. The regimented view of the path ahead when you reach the top (*below*) is stunning in its geometric simplicity.

Chancel Lane Bridge, 1950s and 2012
The nineteenth-century cobbles and latticed bridge sides (*above*) lasted more than half a century, but were replaced in the 1960s with solid brickwork. The ride across may be smoother, but woe betide any motorist foolish enough to stop on those yellow lines!

River Street, 1968 and 2012

Built for Wilmslow's growing workforce, River Street's Victorian terraced houses have been spruced up considerably over the last forty years. Railings removed in the 1940s to assist with the war effort have been replaced, and doors and windows have been renewed. The road surface could still do with some work, though!

**Carrs Park,
c. 1910 and 2012**
Built roughly around
1800, Carrs Mill
produced first cotton,
then silk, and lastly a
type of velvet known
by the remarkably ugly
name of fustian. In 1906
the building became a
laundry, and was then
acquired by brewing
magnate Sir Henry
Boddington, who used it
for storing gelatine until
it burned down in 1923.
Now the site is covered
by lush green swathes
of grass, and children
play in the waters of the
River Bollin.

Carrs Park, 1930 and 2012

Carrs Park is comprised of 70 acres of land acquired over the decades by the local council for the enjoyment of the people of Wilmslow. The earliest donors were the Boddingtons of Pownall Hall in the 1920s, but Silk Mill Cottage (*above*) occupied part of the site in the 1930s, and some of the land was still being used by farmers thirty years later. Today the public-spirited Friends of the Carrs plant native wildflowers and keep an eye on erosion.

Twinnies Bridge, 1900 and 2012
When a lone fisherman sat quietly on the bank beside the graceful arch of Twinnies Bridge in 1900, he could never have dreamt that, 110 years later, a patch of human blood would be found in the car park beyond, unleashing an investigation involving DNA profiling, police dogs and the Cheshire Constabulary helicopter. Happily, the person who lost the blood was pronounced safe and well after a mishap involving no one else, and the bridge resumed its former tranquillity.

Bridges Across the Bollin, 1970 & 2012

Although the more recently built bridges in Carrs Park can't compete with the elegance of Twinnies, they are still appreciated by dog owners, families and solitary walkers as places of quiet contemplation and vantage points for viewing fish, frogs and flowers.

Wilmslow Carnival, 1910, and Silver Jubilee, 1977

Wilmslow Carnival was instituted in 1909 as a more genteel version of the previous century's Wakes processions. The 1910 carnival featured a competition for decorated carts with tableaux of historic and fairytale characters. This hand-coloured Edwardian postcard depicts the rather confusing Red Riding Hood float: which characters, exactly, are all the little girls in white supposed to represent? Presumably it was a case of preventing tears and squabbles by letting them all participate. However, the horse standing between the shafts looks distinctly unimpressed by the unnecessary weight. In Elizabeth II's Silver Jubilee year it was therefore perhaps as well that, like the boat behind, the noble steed in Water Lane was pedal-powered.

Wilmslow Carnival, 1912 and 1979

Horse-drawn floats remained a feature of Wilmslow Carnival for several years, as can be seen from the above photograph of the parade wending its way down Hawthorn Street in 1912. In Water Lane, Scots pipers and drummers in immaculate uniforms were a highlight in the 1970s.

Parades, Early Twentieth Century and 1979

The date of the parade down Hawthorn Street was sadly not recorded, but the long skirts and big hats of the ladies are possibly Edwardian, while the white dresses of the little girls suggest that the celebration was perhaps in honour of May Day. In 1979 it was the turn of young cyclists in sensible hooded coats to take centre stage when rain-washed Water Lane was on the route of the carnival parade.

Marching Bands, 1979 and 1900

The members of Bartholomew's Band gamely played on despite the inclement weather which beleaguered Wilmslow Carnival in 1979. By contrast, parasols and wide-brimmed hats were the order of the day when a brass band serenaded the Sunday school walk through Fulshaw in 1900; maybe the sunshine was a divine reward for faith and virtue...

Hawthorn Hall, 2012 and *c.* 1900

Hawthorn Hall was built in the early seventeenth century by John Latham on land purchased from the Pownall family. Originally timber-framed, it was rebuilt by a subsequent owner, John Leigh, in 1698. In Victorian times it went on to become a boarding school, presided over for forty years by Dr Thomas Somerville. Now screened by mature trees, it's so well camouflaged that only the street name (Hall Road) and the gateposts with their distinctive pine cone finials provide clues to its whereabouts.

Hawthorn Hall, Wilmslow.

Hall Road, Twentieth Century and 2012

Although the precise date of the vintage picture is unknown, it must have been taken a good few decades ago, as Hawthorn Hall is clearly visible from the snow-decked street. Many of the houses on the right were built in the early 1900s. To this day, the road remains a quiet enclave, with vehicular access from Grove Avenue only.

Hawthorn Street, 1890s and 2012

On the 1842 Ordnance Survey map, Hawthorn Street – named after the nearby hall – was called Pepper Street. At the end of the nineteenth century it still had a rustic ambience – and, as every farmer knows, working in the countryside is no picnic. There must have been times when the area's Victorian residents would have loved the convenience of a twenty-first-century Chinese takeaway at the end of a tiring day.

Hawthorn Street, c. 1965 and 2012
Built in 1870, the Methodist New Connexion chapel in Hawthorn Street was demolished amid spectacular clouds of dust the following century. In its place stands Chapel Court, offering sheltered accommodation in twenty-six one-bedroom flats.

Hawthorn Grove, 1920s and 2012

Trees have matured, cars are parked in every drive and some hedges have given way to walls, but otherwise the end of Hawthorn Grove has changed remarkably little over the last ninety years.

Wycliffe Avenue, 1920s and 2012

In the 1920s, a pony and trap was considered the perfect way to view Wycliffe Avenue – at least by this happy mum and toddler if not the stern-faced driver. Nowadays James Bond's wheels of choice dominate the avenue's corner with Water Lane. In neither picture is there any hint of the uproar that occurred in 1940, when an incendiary bomb exploded at Wycliffe Avenue School, injuring two teachers.

Wilmslow Green Room Society, 1947 and 2012

Wilmslow Green Room Society has been entertaining audiences with its theatrical performances since 1924. The earliest photograph in its archive is of a 1947 production of *The Middle Watch*, a comedy featuring, among others, Fred Cookell as father-of-nine Marine Ogg, Margaret Savaage (*sic*) as Mary Carlton, Cedric Keen as Captain Randall and Denovan Nowell as Ah Fong. Its 2012 production of *Steel Magnolias* had a female director and an all-female cast, starring (left to right) Christina Theobald, Lindsey Barker, Mary Cotton, Abby O'Leary and Keeley Chesworth.

Wilmslow Green Room Society, 1972 and 2006

Every summer Wilmslow Green Room Society braves the British weather to give open-air performances against the magnificent backdrop of Gawsworth Hall near Macclesfield. The company's legendary productions of Shakespeare's plays are a particular and timeless favourite, as can be seen from these shots of *Twelfth Night* taken thirty-four years apart.

Department Store, 1950s and 2012

Wilmslow has had its own department store for over fifty years. Until 1982 it was run by Finnegans, which also had a Manchester branch in the 1930s. Like its predecessor, the modern incarnation, Hoopers, specialises in fashion, homeware and beauty products. It has three trading floors and a separate menswear department.

Alderley Road, 1950s and 2012

Alderley Road's shop frontages have been redesigned a few times over the last sixty years to keep pace with shifting consumer tastes. The profile of the flats above, however, would be instantly recognisable to a time-travelling refugee from the 1950s.

Wilmslow Rex, 2012 and 1950s

Run first by Walter Stansby and then his sons Ken and John, Wilmslow Rex celebrated its opening with a gala performance on 15 October 1936. Although best known as a cinema, for forty-nine years it also had a stage, attracting performers like David Jason, Kenneth Williams, Clive Dunn and Wendy Craig. Dwindling audiences led to the Rex's rebirth in 1995 as a combined bookshop, record dealership and cyber-café before its current incarnation as a furniture store. Its iconic Art Deco frontage remains one of Wilmslow's architectural highlights.

THE REX THEATRE AND BUILDINGS, WILMSLOW

Coach and Four, 2012 and 1980s

Acquired by Hydes Brewery from the Greenhall Estate in 1944, the New Inn began life as an eighteenth-century coaching house. Its current name and evocative sign reflect this proud heritage. Window boxes, hanging baskets and Continental-style outdoor tables embellish the frontage, while guests can be accommodated in the adjacent lodge.

Alderley Road, 1900 and 2012
This stretch of Alderley Road leads out to Fulshaw Cross and the main routes to Alderley Edge and Knutsford. Since 1900 buildings have changed, trees have changed and walls have lost railings, making it very hard to gauge the exact spot where the original photographer stood.

Alderley Road, 1900 and 2012

The solitary horse and cart of 1900 has been replaced by cars, the street lamps soar much higher, road signs have been strategically positioned, and the group of long-skirted ladies and children in pinafores has been superseded by a string of cyclists wearing Lycra and helmets; but Alderley Road's glorious trees remain.

Kings Arms, Fulshaw Cross, 2012 and *c.* **1900**

The Kings Arms has been completely rebuilt since its original construction by plumber and glazier Thomas Blower in 1830. A century ago it looked a bit bleak and uninviting, with the maids in their long aprons monitoring proceedings in the doorway, whereas the revamped premises are bright, airy and – menu-wise at least – touched with eastern magic.

Fulshaw Cross, 1900 and 2012
The land in the vicinity of Fulshaw Cross allegedly once belonged to the medieval Knights Hospitaller who offered sanctuary for debtors at their nearby priory. The area was also well-known by Second World War Special Operations Executives (aka spies), who were billeted at Fulshaw Hall during parachute training at Tatton Park and Ringway Airport.

Fire Brigade, Early 1900s and 2012

Wilmslow's first fire station was in Green Lane, but for some reason the brigade – complete with horse-drawn engine – elected to be photographed in front of Fulshaw Hall in the first decade of the twentieth century. From 1909, the crew was based in Hawthorn Street before moving to the £54,000 purpose-built fire station in Altrincham Road in the 1960s. Open days, like the one snapped below, offer the public an opportunity to see the town's fire-fighting equipment and witness the skills of the fire-fighting team.

WE APPRECIATE THE SUPPORT THAT MANY OF YOU HAVE EXPRESSED IN YOUR PHONE CALLS AND VISITS TO OUR STN IN THE PAST 48 HOURS.

RATES BILL

WHAT DOES THE FIRE BRIGADE COST?

LESS THAN 3' IN THE POUND PER YEAR

MERLYN WAVE, YOUR WAND GIVE US A LIVING WAGE

Pickets outside Wilmslow Fire Station.   YW 4601

Fire Brigade, 1978 and 2012

Austerity measures and tightened belts are a recurring feature of British life, and the 1970s in particular were punctuated by various strikes. On the instructions of the Fire Brigades Union, Wilmslow's firemen picketed outside their station in support of a national strike lasting nine weeks. No such dissatisfaction was in evidence at the September 2012 open day, which was regarded as an opportunity to recruit new fire fighters.

Fire Engines, 1950s and 2012
Wilmslow's fire brigade changed from horse-drawn to motorised fire engines in July 1924. The vintage vehicle above belonged to soap and chemical firm Joseph Crosfield of Warrington in the 1950s but is now owned by Cheshire Fire & Rescue. The station tower (*below*) is used for training.

Moor Lane, *c.* 1900 and 2012
Granted, the road surface, yellow lines, signage and satellite dish are all new, but marked similarities remain between the Moor Lane junction of today and yesteryear. The distinctive gable of the shop on the left corner is particularly striking.

Green Hall, Early Twentieth Century and 1960s

Over the centuries Green Hall, nestling in its own grounds, had a succession of owners, including the Hobson family and the Manchester businessman William Paulden, who was commended by the Victorian writer Andrew Pearson for adding 'additional tone and character' with his extensions and renovations. When the premises became the offices of Wilmslow Urban District Council, a rather anachronistic single-storey wing was added to accommodate the public library.

Green Hall, 1978 and 2012

Disaster struck on 9 February 1978, when Green Hall was gutted by fire and had to be demolished. Green Hall Mews – an enclave of two-bedroom flats – rose from the ashes. The terse message on the gate – more off-putting than any council bureaucracy – suggests that sightseers and casual passers-by are cordially unwelcome. Doubtless Messrs Paulden and Pearson would be delighted with the effort to maintain tone.

Library, 1960s and 2012

Wilmslow has a long history of public libraries and reading rooms. In the mid-nineteenth century the village's collection of 300 books was presided over by Jonathan Yarwood, and in 1909 the library shared premises with the fire brigade in Hawthorn Street. The current library was built at the edge of South Drive car park to replace the one damaged in the Green Hall fire. Its facilities include a meeting room which can be hired by the hour.

Library, 1960s and 2012

The stereotypical image of the public library as a dour space with inadequate lighting and strict no-speaking rules may have been applicable forty or fifty years ago, but is no longer remotely accurate. Reading is promoted in its rightful place as a rainbow gateway to adventure, and events like Storytime add a social dimension to library visits.

Romany's Memorial, 1970s and 2012

In the 1930s and '40s, the Methodist minister George Bramwell Evens was better known as Romany of the BBC, a *Children's Hour* broadcaster who gave radio talks about nature. His mother was a full-blood Romany, and he took great delight in holidaying in a gypsy vardo caravan. He retired to Wilmslow in 1939 and died four years later. His vardo was given to the local council and used to be on display outside Wilmslow Library until the decades took their toll and it was sent away for renovation. Whether it will return is uncertain, but the memorials to Romany and his dog Raq can still be seen in a fenced-off area near Wilmslow Library.

Police Station, 1930s and 2012

There has been a police presence in Wilmslow since the nineteenth century, with the number of constables rising from one to four between 1851 and 1881. By then, a superintendent and inspector also swelled the numbers. In the 1930s the police station was in Swan Street, but now the local officers are based at a purpose-built constabulary in the leafy surroundings of Hawthorn Street.

Swan Street, 1890s and 1956

Swan Street was probably named after The Swan, an eighteenth-century coaching inn whose publicans doubled as postmasters. Its horse-drawn vehicles had long given way to the motor car by the 1950s, and somewhere along the way the beautiful old street lamp was sacrificed on the altar of obstacle-free traffic flow – but, apart from a few licks of paint and updated shop signs, the buildings in these pictures look little changed.

Swan Street, 1989 and 2012

By the late 1980s, Swan Street's charm had taken a nosedive, and boarded-up premises awaiting demolition were a sorry sight. In the twenty-first century, Barons Court – the new phoenix on the corner – provides a more attractive vista for motorists waiting at the adjacent traffic lights. Echoing the neck of a brachiosaurus, the lofty street lights are not without allure – but an irrational hankering remains for the Victorian lamp of yesteryear.

Manchester Road, *c.* 1900 and 2012

Time was, you could walk down the centre of Manchester Road at a sedate pace without fear of causing an accident. No chance of that nowadays, hence the slightly different angle of the photograph, taken from the safety of the pavement. Fundamentally unchanged, the houses on the left are a testament to late Georgian construction skills.

Manchester Road, 2012 and Late Nineteenth Century

The presence of this tractor trundling up Manchester Road, at a point just past the view of the church (visible in the vintage picture below), acts as a reminder that, even in the twenty-first century, Wilmslow is embedded in the Cheshire countryside, surrounded by agricultural activities. The building on the right with the hanging baskets is the King William, which has been serving customers for over a century.

Manchester Road/Swan Street Junction, 1930s and 2012

The picture above was taken on the cusp of change. Back Swan Street, the narrow road beside the newsagent's, disappeared in the 1930s, when the building in the centre was also demolished to make way for the current main road. The railings to the left of it once enclosed the Rectory. Latterly, great care has been taken to ensure that redeveloped properties in this area provide an attractive gateway to the town. Links with the past have been maintained by naming the Bollin Fee after the ancient township in which it stands.

Old Rectory, 1956 and 2012

The Old Rectory was built in 1778 for Edward Beresford, Rector of St Bartholomew's parish church. Its dilapidated predecessor had been besieged by Parliamentary forces in the Civil War, resulting in the death of one of the rectory servants. In the 1950s, when the picture above was taken, some of the rectory grounds – originally covering 2 acres – had already been lost to the bypass. The striped swathe of grass is now a cricket pitch.

Old Rectory, 1960s and 2012

By the 1960s, the vines covering the mellow Old Rectory had been stripped away, and it was looking very smart with a fresh white coat of paint. But time marches on and modern-day rectors rarely need to accommodate large families or a sufficient quota of servants to impress the congregation. After a stint as a bank, the building is now a steakhouse 'dripping with rustic charm and original character', according to its website.

Rectory Grounds, 1970s and 2012

The 1970s were a turning-point in the history of the rectory. Its grounds were converted into a beautifully kept playing field, and a leisure centre was built to provide affordable sports facilities for all. The squirrel-emblazoned banner on the leisure centre provides a clue to the land's former use, while the bike-racks are reminiscent of the penny farthings fashionable in the rectory's heyday.

Railway Station, c. 1905 and 2012

In the early twentieth century Wilmslow station incorporated a depot dedicated to handling coal mined at Poynton and Worth Colliery some 7 miles away. Taxis were horse-drawn, and it was possible to loiter in the station approach without fear of being mown down by traffic. No chance of that a century on!

Railway Station, 2012 and 1920s

Originally owned by the Manchester & Birmingham Railway, Wilmslow's station was opened on 10 May 1842 on the Manchester–Crewe line, launching the town's career as commuter-belt. Platform 4, created after the closure of the colliery tracks, is identifiable by the brick wall to the right, but its waiting room now has wheelchair access instead of chimneys. The trains themselves – once pulled by majestic steam engines – are so colourful, they almost look like toys.

STATION·RP·WILMSLOW 755

Station Road, *c.* 1900 and 2012
Looking towards the junction with Manchester Road and Swan Street, Station Road has changed substantially over the decades. The shop in the foreground of the vintage picture was built on the site of a small school endowed by Sir Humphrey de Trafford in 1741, but had to be demolished after falling into disrepair. The wall on the left was once the boundary of the rectory grounds.

Station Road, c. 1900 and 2012

Built around 1860 for the convenience of rail travellers, the Railway Hotel was an imposing and attractive building constructed next to the station at the instigation of William Warham, previously publican of the Ring O' Bells in Church Street. It was demolished after its front garden fell victim to road widening. The site is now occupied by Ladyfield House, designed with considerable architectural flair to provide commercial office space with easy access to Manchester, Crewe and London.

Unitarian Chapel, Dean Row, c. 1900 and 2012

A sign outside Dean Row chapel proclaims that it was established in 1694, but documentary evidence suggests that a Nonconformist congregation began meeting in nearby barns and houses several years earlier. When it was renovated in the 1840s, school rooms were installed at one end and a stable was built in the churchyard for the benefit of worshippers from outlying farms.

Dean Row Unitarian Chapel, 1900 and 2012
If you've ever wondered how much a tree could grow in a century or so, here's your answer... The chapel is almost obscured by foliage and some of the memorials have tilted as the ground beneath has settled, but the unusually tall sundial looks little different.

Dean Row, Early Twentieth Century and 2012
Built to serve as the combined homes and workshops of local handloom silk weavers, these cottages have enjoyed a latter-day renaissance far removed from the cramped existence of the original inhabitants. The end property has not only been decoratively re-thatched, but also extended.

Wesleyan Chapel, Dean Row, Twentieth Century and 2012

Dean Row's Wesleyan chapel was founded in 1799, though the current building was built fifty years later. It continued in use as a place of worship for well over a century. Now it has found new life as a Montessori nursery school.

Altrincham Road, *c.* 1910 and 2012

In 1910 this was the main road from Wilmslow to Altrincham. Now it leads to the M56 as well. Still a mixture of houses and shops – albeit some now untenanted – the buildings on the right have hardly changed in the last hundred years and still face an open patch of tree-decked grass.

Valley Lodge/Holiday Inn, 1970s and 2012

In the 1970s the Valley Lodge – situated in a dip in Altrincham Road – played host to the Cheshire Hunt, which had been formed over 200 years earlier, in 1763. The event depicted was a fox-friendly drag hunt, in which the quarry was a cloth dipped in artificial scent rather than a living, breathing creature. Forty years on, mornings outside the hotel – now the Manchester Airport Holiday Inn – are quieter, and the chances of seeing the sleek lines of a Ford Capri are probably slimmer than a reprise of the drag hunt.

ownall Hall Wilmslow.

Pownall Hall, 1910s and 2012

Built in the 1830s and altered fifty years later in response to the fashionable Arts and Crafts movement, Pownall Hall was named after its owner, James Pownall of Liverpool, who demolished a medieval manor house to make way for it. In 1885 it became the home of Manchester brewing magnate Henry Boddington before being converted into a private school.

Pownall Hall, Twentieth Century and 2012
Tarmac, brick pillars, wire fencing and signs banning smoking, dogs and traffic travelling at more than 5 mph – that's what happens to mellow entrance gates when a private residence becomes a school.

Pownall Park, *c.* 1902 and 2012

The elegantly attired ladies in the distance are strolling down Carrwood Road, with Pownall
Hall to the left. The modern picture was taken further down the lane, which emerges opposite
Wilmslow Rugby Union Football Club. As the rugby club has been going strong since 1884, it
is entertaining – though probably apocryphal – to imagine that the ladies were off for a spot of
refined Edwardian cheerleading.

Broadwalk, Pownall Park, 1970s and 2012

In the 1930s Wilmslow's Pownall Park suburb was built on land which had been owned by Richard de Pounale back in the thirteenth century. A few trees have had to be felled since the earlier photograph was taken, but the spacious avenue retains a prosperous air. One mystery though – should Broadwalk be one word or two? The street signs vary...

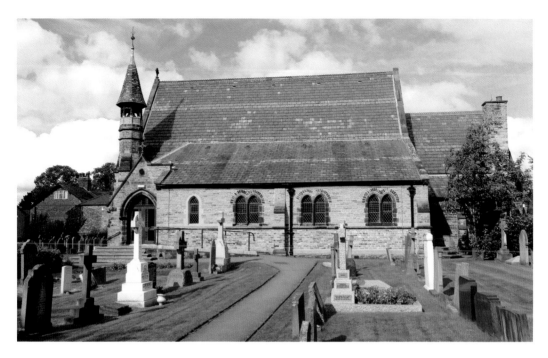

St John's Church, Lindow, 2012 and Twentieth Century

The church of St John the Evangelist was built in 1873/74 to cater for Wilmslow's growing population as it moved outwards from its traditional core, resulting in the formation of a brand-new parish: Lindow St John. Since then, the church's main entrance has been redesigned, the roofline has changed, a neat path has taken the place of greensward, and the number of graves has inevitably increased.

Lindow, 1905 and 2012

Sadly, the artistry and skill of the past cannot always be matched. Despite several attempts, I was unable to locate the spectacular line of trees (*above*), superbly photographed by T. Baddeley in December 1905. On a sunny September day 107 years on, the nearest equivalent I could capture of a half-screened house in Lindow was the vista below and right. The poplars are glorious, but my shots undeniably lack the dramatic impact of Mr Baddeley's.

Lindow Common, 2012 and 1870s

The picture of Lindow Common below is one of the earliest surviving photographs of the Wilmslow area. Now only a tenth of its original size, the common was a treacherous, bog-laden expanse where vipers lurked and men and cattle sometimes drowned. It was plagued by gnats, and enclosed in 1777, but neither factor stopped gypsies and tinkers camping on its inhospitable terrain – note the caravan beyond the lake.

Lindow Common, *c.* 1900, 1956 and 2012
Black Lake was formed in the late glacial period when streams merged with melting blocks of ice. In the 1950s, people were allowed to go canoeing and rowing there, and in Edwardian times a cold snap (*inset*) offered the chance to go skating. Neither activity is possible at Lindow in the safety-conscious, 'please-don't-sue-us' twenty-first century. The lake is now ringed by fencing, leaving ducks to dominate the surface.

Lindow Locals, Iron Age, 1974 and 2012

Literally cut down in his prime, Britain's most famous Iron Age sacrificial victim (*inset*) was hit twice on the skull and garrotted before having his throat cut and being thrust face-down into a pool. He was found in Lindow Moss a decade after the peat cutters above were photographed harvesting their crop. Nowadays the common is a favourite leisure spot where children play and dog-walkers live long, happy lives. Who knows? Perhaps their future was secured by Lindow Man's act of propitiation...